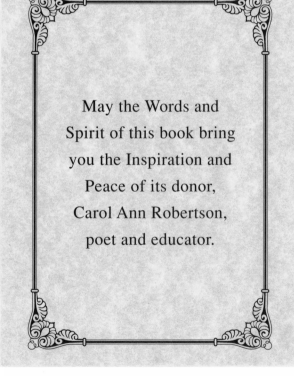

May the Words and
Spirit of this book bring
you the Inspiration and
Peace of its donor,
Carol Ann Robertson,
poet and educator.

Dark Horses

Johns Hopkins: Poetry and Fiction
John T. Irwin, General Editor

X. J. Kennedy

Dark
Horses

NEW POEMS

The Johns Hopkins University Press
Baltimore and London

This book has been brought to publication with the
generous assistance of the Albert Dowling Trust.

The Johns Hopkins University Press
701 West 40th Street
Baltimore, Maryland 21211-2190
The Johns Hopkins Press Ltd., London

Library of Congress Cataloging-in-Publication Data

Kennedy, X. J.
    Dark horses : new poems / X. J. Kennedy.
        p.   cm. — (Johns Hopkins, poetry and fiction)
    ISBN 0-8018-4484-3 (HC). — ISBN 0-8018-4485-1 (PBK)
    I. Title.   II. Series.
PS3521.E563D3   1992
811'.54—dc20   92-10014

Once again, for Dorothy

Contents

I

Woman in Rain

Down brimming streets she walks, the bole
Of a young tree uprooted whole,
    Impelled along a breakneck flood
    Of rushing traffic, flesh and blood.

Sleek taxis on the prowl for cash
Through overflowing potholes bash—
    She dodges sheets of water, steps
    Past handbills (DEEP MASSAGE—TRY SHEP'S)

And, twained by her determined stride,
The strings of rain to strands divide,
    A beaded curtain, thin and blue.
    She parts its danglings, steps on through

To farther rooms, still unaware
That she as we behold her there
    Might grace a page or fill a frame.
    But then, what planet knows its name?

The Arm

A day like any natural summer day
Of hide-and-seek along the river shore,
Till Snaker, probing with a snapped-off bough,
Dredged up the severed arm,
Let out a shout of glee
And shook it in my face like some grim charm.

In nightmare even now,
Dribbling dark bottom-ooze,
Those fingers green with algae, infantile,
Reach out as though to fasten hold on me—
I turned and ran, abandoning my shoes,
Snaker and that little horror at my heels.

Was it a bit of flesh
Or only rubber wrenched loose from some doll
Who died and bit the trash? I never knew,
But that it couldn't fasten on at will
Made sense. And so I tried
Not fearing it, tried all night long, but still

Night after night the arm,
Joined to a wrinkled baby with no nose
And cratered eyes would tap my windowpane,
Its cries squeezed shrill from trying to break through:
Why do you leave me out here in the rain?
It's dark and cold. Let me come sleep with you.

Twelve Dead, Hundreds Homeless

The wind last night kept breaking into song—
Not a song, though, to comfort children by.
It picked up houses, flung them down awry,
Upended bridges, drove slow trees along
To walls.
        A note so high
Removed an ear that listened. On the strand
Without a word this morning, sailors land.
White cars, their sirens off, wade silently.

Now crews inch by, restringing power lines,
Plowing aside the sparkling drifts of glass.
The wind last night kept breaking into song
Beautiful only if you heard it wrong.

Fall. You're driving 84 southwest—
A hillock scarlet as a side of beef
Accosts your eyes. Gigantic on its crest,
An outstretched cross stands waiting for its thief.

Your fingers as though hammered to the wheel
Clench hard. Frost-kindled sumac blazes down
Like true gore pouring from a bogus crown.
The earth grows drizzled, dazzled, and bedrenched.

Did even Wallace Stevens at the last,
Having sown all his philosophe's wild oats,
Gape for the sacred wafer and clutch fast
To Mother Church's swaddling petticoats?

Connecticut's conversions stun. Is there
Still a pale Christ who clings to hope for me,
Who bides time in a cloud? Choking, my car
Walks over water, across to Danbury.

For Jed

It wastes us all, Jed, you
More quickly than the rest.
Posted in your ward bed,
You watch carnations fail
In the tumbler of water we
Freshen, although you seldom
Ask for a drink. You front
A Great Ming Wall of boredom.

Battling at chess with Katz,
The cancerous pants-presser,
You hoist lance for your knight
While, outdoors, evening hovers
Like poisoned doves. Stand guard
On your state of quilted covers.
No one, nobody human
Stays immune forever.

Veterinarian

Terrified bleat, bellow and hoofbeat, thrash,
She quiets with black bag. Working alone
On hands and knees, a carpenter of flesh,
She joins together staves of broken bone,
Mends fences for the bloodstream that would run
Out of the raving dog, the shattered horse,
Her hands as sure as planets in their course.

Now prestidigitates before the wide-
Eyed children without trying to, intent
On tugging forth a live calf from the bride
Of the bull, bandages the brood mare's ligament.
Now by her labor arteries are bent,
Grappled, tied fast like saplings under duress.
She murmurs words to soothe the languageless.

Leaves like a plowman order in her wake.
Home for a hot tub and a single feast
Of last night's pizza, watching cold dawn break,
Knowing that some will live—a few, at least—
Though foam-jawed, wild-eyed, the eternal beast
Annihilation with perpetual neigh
Takes worlds like ours with water twice a day.

Bitter Man

From birth screwed tight, I writhed inside my soul.
Now like a screw I fill a twisted hole.

Preacher

Too late. The Hell I threatened cannot hurt you.
The wordless worm best knows how to convert you.

Anyman

Friend, though you call, you shall not find me in.
My tombstone? A mere answering machine.

Misanthrope

Does misery love company? So they say.
But how am I in misery? Keep away.

Attorney

In compost lying low, composed in face,
I scribble briefs for Jesus, just in case.

Lecher

I who could once erect a throbbing bone
Salute you now with rigid, skinned-back stone.

Watchmaker

And here you stand and stare while minutes fly.
Time lessens you. But even less am I.

Writer

I who once dealt in words and set great store
On words have, in a word or two, no more.

Anyman Again

Friend, you are only one. Whole hordes have died.
Why try to fight? The odds are on our side.

Kicking and shrieking off to bed,
   Hand tugged in the Lord God's hand,
He fought as he always did
   When day had to end.

The animals you eat
Leave footprints in your eyes.
You stare, four-year-old pools
Troubled. "They don't have souls,"
I tell you, in defeat.

Has no one ever dined
In bedtime stories pink
Cuddlable pigs inhabit,
No one stewed Peter Rabbit
In that land of pure mind?

You tinker with your burger,
Doubtful. "It doesn't matter,"
I say. We kill by proxy
And so, like Foxy Loxy,
Dissemble while we murder.

"Lambs wouldn't have a life
Romping in black-eyed Susans
If they weren't to be eaten."
But your lip quivers. Beaten,
I'm caught with dripping knife.

To bed now. Gravely wise,
You face night on your own.
I smooth your pillow and sheet.
The animals you eat
Start turning to your eyes.

Snug

What, dead? Aunt Edith, whom the children dubbed
　　The Bug behind her back? Have limp hands dropped
　　　　That sheaf of metered mail
　　　　She'd leaf through for live letters? Have her frail
　　Clock-stockinged legs, now done with running, stopped?

How shall we do without her seasonal
　　Flutter of air through rudiments of wings,
　　　　Her stay announced for "at most, fourteen days"
　　　　(Oh, never less), her ladybirdlike ways
　　Of scurry, scamper, scoot—of fondling things

In several-focaled insect spectacles?
　　Preoccupied with faint but useful service—
　　　　Polishing nutpicks, Wooliting toy lambs' fleece,
　　　　Giving each pillowcase a keener crease—
　　She'd do her best to please. Yet make us nervous.

What care she gave to gently folding things,
    To children, creatures—questing, we now see,
        Some borrowed resting place, as beetles who,
        Needing some knot of comfort to undo,
    Couch in the center of a peony.

Can it be that near evening, after all,
    The earth begrudged her scurrying brief stay?
        Hardly. Inter The Bug
        In that prim chrome-clasped touring bag she'd lug
    When, wings part-warmed, she'd poise to skim away.

Invasion and Retreat

being a recollection of a voyage
to and from Manhattan by Barclay Street ferry

Roast coffee in the nostrils strove to blend
    With violets cropped. Walls scabrous with disease
    Of torn election posters fended cries
From creaking gulls, pushcarters out to vend,
    Fish-filleters who swore in Portuguese.

My plan to storm New York died in midcharge —
    I cruised home. In reflection still repose
    Swayed waters, that intensity of rose
With which the sun, transforming tug and barge,
    Captured Hoboken's archipelagoes.

Where the sea has more blue shades than Eskimo
Has names, it's said, for different kinds of snow,
Undulant palm fonds emulate each wave.
Liners pour shots of crowd. Men rush to save
On liquor at the dockside mall. Their wives
Glance at their throats and finger Swedish knives.
Hill-perched, the Hotel Eighteen Twenty-nine
Endures a crux: a waiter dribbles wine
Into a diner's lap. A swooping corm-
Orant beaks prey. Operation Desert Storm
Crackles through static as our driver veers
To spare a goat. The war!—we prick up ears
Like mute agnostics straining to believe.
Iraqi missiles riddle Tel Aviv
And far-off sandclouds struggle to abort
Air missions. Willard Scott has the report
On Saudi weather. Here, rain clouds congeal,
Drain for a minute, stop. This land's surreal

Yet violent: When rum-distilling Danes
Imported human cargo packed in chains,
Defiance summoned quick official wrath
For the quelled rebels. In its aftermath,
The French commander merely for the sake
Of good form had six judged. Three died at stake,
One sizzled slowly, one was sawed in half,
A third impaled, his head stuck on a staff
In seventeen thirty-four. Old stuff. Although
In this calm tourist harbor, months ago,
We're told, along one hurricane-torn street
Folks tossed small coins before the stumbling feet
Of a blind Jew, blood seeping from his head—
Bets on how long he'd take to fall down dead.
Today the sun dives in a copper blaze
To vanish as if flushed beyond lush cays
Where old resentments gather to a boil
Fueled by "white gold"—that's us. The Persian Gulf
Lies slicked in oil.

The front had such a rutted look
That on the move through hers
You seemed to ford streams, mount hills thick
And dark with tufted firs.

A lone bulb's eyeball by her bed
Lit roads in disrepair
Yet regiments came scatheless through
The barbed wire of her hair,

Up from her body's stony trench
Where many a private crept,
Ducked for a while the kiss of shell
And caught his breath and slept.

Two from Apollinaire

1   *Pont Mirabeau*

Under Pont Mirabeau glides the Seine
      And loves of ours
   Must I think back to when
Joy always followed in the wake of pain

         Sound the hour   night draw near
         The days go running   I stay here

Hand in my hand stand by me face to face
      While underneath
   The bridge of our embrace
Weary of everlasting looks the slow wave passes

         Sound the hour   night draw near
         The days go running   I stay here

Love flows away as running water went
    Love flows away
  As life is indolent
And as Hope is   violent

     Sound the hour   night draw near
     The days go running   I stay here

Though days run on   though days and weeks run on
    No time gone by
  No love comes back again
Under Pont Mirabeau glides the Seine

     Sound the hour   night draw near
     The days go running   I stay here

2 Churchbells

Gypsy tall dark my lover
Listen the churchbells sound
We loved each other and got lost
Not dreaming we'd be found

But we were badly covered up
Now every bell has spied
Our secret from its steepletop
And spilled it villagewide

Tomorrow Cyprien and Henri
Catherine and Marie Ursule
The baker's wife the baker
And Cousin Gertrude all

Will smile at me when I walk by
I won't know where to lay me
You'll by far from my side I'll cry
And that will kill me maybe

In shadowland you learn to wear
A doublebreasted shadow suit,
A mask for when you venture out.
You sleep, flesh draped across a chair.

To stand up straight you have to bend.
You jump, your path crossed by a cat.
You start awake when telephones
Clang from the floor above your flat

As though the light of day could bring
The clocklike latch, unlatch of arms
While in a thousand basement rooms
Your thoughts explode like fire alarms.

Terse Elegy for J. V. Cunningham

Now Cunningham, who rhymed by fits and starts,
So loath to gush, most sensitive of hearts—
Else why so hard-forged a protective crust?—
Is brought down to the unresponding dust.
Though with a slash a Pomp's gut he could slit,
On his own flesh he worked his weaponed wit
And penned with patient skill and lore immense,
Prodigious mind, keen ear, rare common sense,
Only those words he could crush down no more
Like matter pressured to a dwarf star's core.
May one day eyes unborn wake to esteem
His steady, baleful, solitary gleam.
Poets may come whose work more quickly strikes
Love, and yet—ah, who'll live to see his likes?

Long Distance

Desperate poets call you late at night
To ask what's wrong, why editors resist
The moistened lips they thrust up to be kissed.

One reads a villanelle you'll love. The phone
Oozing warm blood, you listen. Pillow talk.
The more he reads the more, outside, winds moan.

You stammer, Yeah, you've got an ear there, kid.
Only, did you ever think—well, how about
Not just redoing what the Georgians did?

Dead air. A hard laugh barricades his anger.
He thanks you for your time. He'll call again.
Sure, any time, you say. You hang up. Rain
Strums on the roof with amputated finger.

Between posts, two on either shore,
A bridge once stood that is no more
And what had it left to bequeath
But four blunt stumps like snapped-off teeth.

The shores reflect with frozen glare
A changing river. Did it wear,
Their constant nearness, till, long lulled,
They woke to find all bonds annulled?

It seems as if both sides await
Some last division of estate
Or kind winds from a civil court
To shake one down for nonsupport,

But all that walks forth to be seen
On emptiness, a go-between
Too tentative to make amends,
Is one wan oak leaf at loose ends

And where's true compromise in such
A slight attempt to keep in touch?
Neither owns up to being wrong
And so they stand and stand and long.

No, I am witless. Often in despair
At long-worked botches crumpled, thrown away—
A few lines worth the keeping, all too rare.
Blind chance not wit entices words to stay
And recognizing luck is artifice
That comes unlearned. The rest is taking pride
In daily labor. This and only this.
On keyboards sweat alone makes fingers glide.

Witless, that juggler rich in discipline
Who brought the Christchild all he had for gift,
Flat on his back with beatific grin
Keeping six slow-revolving balls aloft;
Witless, La Tour, that painter none too bright,
His draftsman's compass waiting in the wings,
Measuring how a lantern stages light
Until a dark room overflows with rings.

II

On the Liquidation of the Mustang Ranch by the Internal Revenue Service

This poor old spread, its waterholes turned dust,
    Its paying herd stampeded, lies here slain.
    On Reno's rock-shanked hills frustrated rain
Refuses to descend. Spangles of rust
Bestride the bar where hands no longer shake
    Quick daiquiris to blur the fear of AIDS,
    Net stockings dangle hollow, grand parades
Kick off no more. A hibernating snake

Lies not more still. Beneath the auctioneer's
    Gavel fall crates of condoms, lingerie,
        The sign from the mirrored orgy chamber: FIRE
EXIT, the kindly tank of oxygen
        Whose sweet breath could that reveler inspire
    To flare, who might have smoldered in dismay.

Lying in bed till late, she watched her dreams
Drizzle to daydreams and dissolve to thought,
But thought that had what thought ought not have: knots.

From the bricked alley came the shriek of drums,
Brakedrums, bringing to an abrupt stop
The express truck delivering a new Book-of-the-Month
Too early. Crème de Menthe
In the glass used to marinate by night
Her dentures helped.
                    The day, precise and green,
Curled, a possessive cat, upon the spread,
Stared hard at her, not knowing what to mean,
Preparing for a hurtle through her head.

Song: Enlightenment

> The elephant selected to carry what is believed to be the
> tooth of Buddha in an annual festival has arrived in Colombo
> en route to his new home at Sri Lanka's holiest shrine.
>
> News dispatch

It takes a two-ton elephant with a bobbing teak
    telephone booth
Resplendent with gold to aspire to hold the Gautama
    Buddha's tooth.
Hear the bong of the gong and the sigh as the throng
    of worshipers whooshes aside
Like a bowing grain-row that that tooth may go and
    its grandiose pachyderm stride.

Now you or I lose a tooth and cry when the twisting
    pliers unplug
An ache from our chops and the dentist plops it into
    his stainless steel jug,
And nobody prays on our holy days to a scrap of our
    castoff bone,
Nor do we aspire to a hymning choir, nor seek to fix
    teeth on a throne.

Yet enlightenment comes not from banging drums,
    nor from giving prayer wheels a whiz,
But by realizing just what the surprising fact of the
    matter is:
It can strike like the jolt of a billion-volt bolt and leave
    one a bit the wiser,
Knowing any old tooth as immense in truth as that
    elephant-borne incisor.

Speculating Woman

Left in the lurch, I found the will
To bed down with a dollar bill
And soon forgot love's brief alarms
In Grover Cleveland's rustling arms.
A constant eight per cent more fond
I grew in that new marriage bond
And every new year thanked the Lord
For fresh increase and well-chaired board.

Unlike grown daughters, dividends
Make no pretense to be your friends
Nor ever give you cause to doubt
Whose hands they're in when they go out.
What mortal husband do you know
Whose interest each month will grow?
See, women, how those mates of yours
Depreciate. While mine endures.

Drawn round the roasting of a bird
   By duty once each year,
With first a drink and soon a third,
   They baste glazed looks of cheer.

Each spine erected in its seat,
   Each head bowed low for grace,
All wait the word to fork white meat
   In through the family face.

Emily Dickinson Leaves a Message to the World,
Now That Her Homestead in Amherst Has an Answering Machine

Because I could not stop for Breath

Past Altitudes – of Earth –

Upon a reel of Tape I leave

Directions to my Hearth –

For All who will not let me lie

Unruffled in escape –

Speak quickly – or I'll intercept

Your Message with – a Beep.

Though often I had dialed and rung

The Bastion of the Bee –

The Answer I had hungered for

Was seldom Home – to me –

Dancing with the Poets at Piggy's

for Alan Dugan

When cold winds grasp it, Provincetown
    At last can be afforded:
Tall summer rents come tumbling down,
    Boutiques sit numbly boarded,

The lobster hones its tinshear claws,
    The scent of pot wafts fainter,
The beachboys' tidal wave withdraws,
    In flows the method painter.

In wintertime in Provincetown
    Strict meter's old and mealy,
Closed wharves lie cold, green hulls grow mold,
    The fog's Eugene O'Neilly.

God guard us from the mind alone!
    When thought grows stiff and wiggy
And blank white sheets stare poets down,
    We'll go shake butt with Piggy.

I showed up at a poet's pad
  To view her new collection—
Beneath her bedsheet lay a lad
  With tentpole-like erection

And all the while I'd criticize
  Each faintly labored measure,
Resentfully from bed, his sighs
  Protested postponed pleasure.

At Piggy's, once The Pilgrim Club,
  Sand, sleet and sea-salt mingle,
The beachplum wrinkles on its shrub,
  The beach hangs out its shingle,

And in that dim upholstered sty
  Plump rumps revolve in rhythm
While watching, quickly aging, I
  Sip tepid Pabst Blue Ribbon.

Says Dugan, bard, to Kennedy
   As smoke and senses thicken,
Yuh take young lovers where yuh teach?—
Say I, *Not me, I'm chicken,*

   And when beside a fount of love
      Who overflows his basin
Man lies each night, to poke and shove
      Some callow girl why hasten?

Now darkness gathers force and climbs,
   Rock-harder grows the rhythm.
In roiling deeps the lost line swims
   That takes a life to fathom.

By beats too throbbing to ignore
   I'm roused to emulation
Till, dragging carcass to the floor,
   I essay a gyration.

One piddling flake of snow swoops in.
   Beams creak, a floorboard buckles,
The dancers swivel hams again—
   What raps with meatless knuckles?

At Piggy's out in Provincetown
   The day dissolves its traces
And few words end up written down
   But what salt tide erases.

III

Rat

Strolling to Mass. General Hospital
For her radiation treatment,
She passed by Suffolk County Jail.
On the pavement lay a beaten

Rat, gray and red. Had a prisoner
Arrested it by the fur,
Knocked out its brain against a wall
And flung it through the bars?

Which thought thrust her, strangely, into cheer:
That someone trapped had to be
Locked up inside with a scampering brood
While she in the sun walked free—

And though a beast with pinpoint teeth
Scurried in her own shadow,
She felt at one with that urge to kill
And throw out and clean house.

The homeless on the sidewalk said
As we walked by, *Wish I was dead?*—

And sat back in his self-made pond
Of piss. Your eyes flashed, *Don't respond,*

And so the quarter in my hand
I'd meant to toss him did not land.

Denying him, I felt denied
A swig from that brown-bagged bottle, pride.

Circling the walk
Where rusty benches on scaled birdlegs perch,
Competing for one kernel, wings alurch,
    Two he-males stalk.

Neither will acquiesce.
Blue beak-tipped arrow, one dives for the other,
Grasps and removes some neck-fluff. Whorls of feather
    Phosphoresce.

Slowly as if in dream,
A dealer in crack unjackknifes from a bench,
Twitches numb muscles, makes stiff fingers clench,
    A switchblade gleam

In his right hand, to sway
Over a huge-eyed boy: "You holdin' out
On me. You took in pretty near about
    Eight hundred, say?"

The hireling's shrugs default
His contract obligation. Straight down swings
The blade—its edge bites feelinglessly, slings
        Blood to asphalt.

        Now like a wine-
Skin pierced, the body in its outrush veers
To earth. The dealer pivots, disappears.
        A siren mourns.

        The boy is let to lie
Mouth open, draining. Like a funeral barge,
A stately stretcher comes. Nurse tugs her charge
        Home lest she testify.

        Meanwhile, at one remove,
From the cool eaves of the urinal
Plump hens with throats of umber, breasts of coral,
        Flute and approve.

City-Quitter

Down inbound Ninety-three, straight route that wings
To bullseye Boston through concentric rings
Of ringroads, faster than the sun can drive,
Young brokers from New Hampshire farms arrive
Like thudding arrows at the Charlesbank merge,
Painstakingly inch forward to converge
In three contending lanes. The city's gate
Presents a truck to circumnavigate
That's slimed the road with shells and scrambled eggs:
Others' mishaps, to savor to the dregs.

The city's where it's at: this traffic crunch,
Craftshops, theaters, being stood to lunch,
Cop sirens and the subtly lurking fear
Of slashers' blades, the changing of the year
That hatches fresh-fledged swanboats in the park—
And yet I've opted for the outer dark:

A stand of maples, squirrelcalls, running-room
For children, boredom. I embrace my doom—
Outbound to Alewife! On a Red Line train
I rocket to that still point where the chain
Of burbs commences at a brook once rife
With agile food fish named for some good wife,
Now crammed with trucks and taxicabs. But soon
The hills of Lexington accept a moon
Drawn like a bow, and gunning engine, I
Am driven to a safer place to die
Where privacies are clung to like beliefs
And separate houses wall in separate griefs.

The homeowners, gone to the Cape,
    Have instructed their house to exude
Ninety minutes of Mozart on tape—
    But what magic flute can delude

The dimmest-brained housebreaker? Light,
    Precisely as ordered to, glows
From dusk till eleven at night,
    At which digital clockstroke those

Who neither consume nor cast shade
    Behind the drawn blinds of their cell
Into beds that stay creaselessly made
    Have to slide, impalpable,

In a mansion computer-programmed
    To make threatening noise: a machine
For confining the souls of those damned
    To a heaven of perfect routine.

The Woodpile Skull

Not one now to mock your own
grinning? quite chop-fallen?

A log I took for one more log to stack
Spills from my arms and, sprawling on its back,
Drops from its face a black ant's severed head,
Jaws pincered round a crumb of hardwood bread.
I pick it up. It and its viselike grip
Weigh next to nothing on my fingertip—
To think a neck this slight could so hold steady
A whole oak till its overthrow got ready.

How did my chainsaw know enough to bite
With such precision? Tumbrils in the night
Could not have trundled to a guillotine
A marquis for a severing more clean.
I doubt he'd meant so faithfully to stand,
Just failed to hear his regiment disband,
Clinging to duty like some primitive
Who feels beneath his feet a tundra give
In to a tar pit and, before he wists,
Wakes to the spades of archeologists.

This dying, though a country mile from great,
Leads me to think less of whatever Fate
Parts heads from shoulders with indifference,
Decrees the moment of our going hence.
I wouldn't put it past Their Enmities
To thin us out as winter winnows trees
With sudden unpremeditated blows
And bask in comfort from our overthrows.

Wind wedges through my woodpile. But this chill
Comes from a sense that, blindly, I can kill
And can be killed. Bemused and metaphoric,
I stand, ham Hamlet to a formic Yorick.

Dump

The brink over which we pour
Odd items we can't find
Enough cubic inches to store
In house, in mind,

Is come to by a clamber
Up steep unsteady heights
Of beds without a dreamer
And lamps that no hand lights.

Here lie discarded hopes
That hard facts had to rout:
Umbrellas—naked spokes
By wind jerked inside-out,

Roof-shingles bought on sale
That rotted on their roof,
Paintings eternally stale
That, hung, remained aloof,

Pink dolls with skulls half-crushed,
Eyes petrified in sleep—
We cast off with a crash
What gives us pain to keep.

As we turn to return
To a lightened living room,
The acrid smell of trash
Arises like perfume.

Maneuvering steep stairs
Of bedsprings to our car,
We stumble on homecanned pears
Grown poisonous in their jar

And nearly gash an ankle
Against a shard of glass.
Our emptiness may rankle,
But soon it too will pass.

Summer Children

These summer children, quickly made
In marriages that came undone,
Exchange tin shovels. Up from sand
They palm-press walls against the waves.
What currents do they understand?

Like creaking-pulley gulls, they quarrel—
They've taken too much sun today.
Now foam consumes their castle keep,
Draping their towels with sodden laurel.
Children, it's high time. Come away.

Concussions of the surf resound
As though in shells. Once sunken deep,
Like driftwood a September chill
Rises, returns. From summers gone,
These children may be all we keep.

Tableau Intime

The thin-chinned girl diagnosed as hyperactive
Curls in a heap on the couch, limp from the rebuke
Of her large mother who stands imploring, "Practice,
Damn you, practice your violin." A stream of puke

Pours from her mother's live-in lover's lips
Into the toilet crock at which he kneels,
A penitent communicant. Froth drips,
Spins down the drain. His feet regained, he wheels

Back to the parlor, balances the couch
With his slumped weight. Cora kicks off her shoes,
Seizes the cheap, neglected violin,
Scrapes out a dissonance. "Can't hold your booze?"

She jeers. The lover eyes her with disdain,
Aims a sharp swing but misses. "Ma!" she shrills,
"Ma, stop him! Fritz is hitting me again—
He's always hitting me." "Time for your pills,"

Calls Mother, reappearing with two bottles,
Capsules for Cora, Four Roses straight for Fritz.
Stunned by a bounding shoe, in its waterless bowl
The old paint-mottled pet turtle collects its wits.

Now death has hooked his stocking on the tree
In the shocked house where branches tilt and break
Under the weight of his fulfilled request.
Soon there will be
As though it had been set down by mistake
One walnut package longer than the rest.

The children take each plastic Wise Man down
To tissuewrap him, stall him in his box.
They do not see
The common sense in stripping bare their tree
So soon, where lights revolved like carousels
And cool steel stars came needling through a sky
Of tensile boughs where Kringles made of tin,
Inhuman things that cast a silver sheen,
That gave and gave and never could deny
Sleighed on and on, across the evergreen.

Staring into a River Till Moved by It

Down bedrock rails the river shot,
   Scattering pebbles. As it went,
The bridge we stood on lost in thought
   Broke from its shoulders of cement

And backwards made off with our looks,
   Resistless as a ship departs.
As if some knife had twained our necks,
   No heads stood lookout for our hearts.

How many minutes channeled past
   We did not know. It seemed we roared
At breakneck speed though still moored fast,
   Too rooted to jump overboard.

But day wore on. Two staterooms burned
   Back of our porthole's bolted blinds.
Our thoughts to even keel returned
   And leveling, ballasted our minds.

Inert, your hand dropped from my hand.
 Unbudged, rocks in the stream stood
And as we dragged our shoes to land
  The drydocked trees raised hulls of wood.

The third time I submerged,
I couldn't see to drown.
Salt bit my eyes. There broke
A breaker in my mind.

What did I see down there,
Nosing the numb fish
And after, flung upon
Shells with their clappers gone?

Nothing but weeds that made
A clear stair dwindling down,
One claw like a doll's hand
Turning, end over end—

Under the surface swirl
Of contending foam,
White veins in green marble,
The deep stood full as stone.

Finis

Like an ice swan, the party melts. It's late.
Karen calls names, Blanche falls to yanking hair.
Wadded and blown through straws, the cake in bullets
Splatters, grape Kool-Aid puddles every chair,
Fudge sauce eats through each sodden paper plate.

Vision begins to shimmer—are you dreaming?
Like a tired child impatient parents drag
Out to the car you're strong-armed, all your winnings
Clutched in a little star-decked paper bag.
It's cold, it's growing dark. You go off screaming.

Black Velvet Art

On a corner in rainriddled Lewiston blooms a stand
Of giant paintings, guaranteed made by hand:
Elvis with hairdo laced with bright gold nimbus,
Jesus with heart aflame, arms wide to bless
Your pickup truck, a leopard crouched to leap
Upon a bathing beauty sound asleep,
And all resplendent on a jet-deep back-
Ground of profoundly interstellar black,
Blacker than nearby space,
So that these cat-toothed hues spring to deface
Eyes disbelieving. Gaseous scrimmages
Of car and bus gun by these images
Here blossomed where the Androscoggin flows
Between banks that sprout work socks and cheap shoes,
Where old men hark back to that glory day
When Liston took a dive for Cassius Clay.

That corner bears news of a world apart
From this one. Two-for-fifteen-dollar art
Fulfills a need not known, for which we yearn
Unwittingly. The next day we return
To find all wonder banished,
The pavement gray and blank, its gallery vanished
Like stars at that final dawn when God commands
Even the last black hole, *Get off My Hands*.

Winter Thunder

The two of us at odds in numb December
Hear overhead the widening crack of thunder
As though, we huddling in our separate cells,
Juggling our tin trays piled with gristly rations,
A friendly dynamite works its detonations
And in a flash our jailblock breaks and falls.

Ambition

First blow of October, and oak leaves shy
Down from branches they value not overly high
As though to cast off at a breath of cold
Were as easy as hanging on, gathering gold.

Their casualness ravishes. Was I wrong
To have clung to my workdesk the summer long,
Scratching out, striving? What now to show
But dread of the coming of drifted snow?

I'd be glad to go out on a limb with those
Who can live with whatever the wind bestows
Were it not for these roots, dug in deep to bear
Never being done grasping for light and air.

Acknowledgments

"On the Liquidation of the Mustang Ranch by the Internal Revenue Service" first appeared in *The Atlantic*; "Emily Dickinson Leaves a Message to the World" and "The Woodpile Skull," in *Chronicles*; "Ambition," in *Cumberland Poetry Review*; "Family Reunion," in *The Epigrammatist*; "The Arm," in *Erato / Harvard Book Review*; "Separated Banks," in *The Formalist*; "Summer Children," in *Four Quarters*: "The Animals You Eat" and "Invasion and Retreat," in *Gramercy Review* (in a metrical poetry issue edited by Henri Coulette); "Tableau Intime," in *Kentucky Poetry Review* (in a number dedicated to Dabney Stuart); "Dancing with the Poets at Piggy's," in *Laurel Review*; "Empty House Singing to Itself," in *The Nation*; "Terse Elegy of J. V. Cunningham" and "Twelve Dead, Hundreds Homeless," in *The New Criterion*; "Song: Enlightenment," in *The New York Quarterly*; "Winter Thunder," in *The Northern Review*; "Coming Close to Drowning" and "To the Writers Forbidden to Write," in *The North Stone Review*; "Dump," "On the Square," "Rat," "War Newscast in St. Thomas," and "The Waterbury Cross," in *Ontario Review*; "Finis," in *Open Places*; "Veterinarian," in *Paintbrush*; "City-Quitter," in *Pivot*; "Staring into a River Till Moved by It," in *Poem*; "City Churchyard" and "On Being Accused of Wit," in *Poetry*; "For Jed," in *Poets for Life: Seventy-six Poets Respond to AIDS*, edited by Michael Klein (Crown

Publishers); "Overnight Pass," in *Radix*; "Long Distance," in *Redstart Plus*; "For a Small Boy's Stone" and "Woman in Rain," in *Scarecrow*; "Black Velvet Art" and "Snug," in *The Sewanee Review*; "Speculating Woman," in *Spectrum*; "Rotten Reveille," in *Stray Dog*; and "Christmas Abrupted," in *The Western Poet*.

Many of these items have been rewritten or retitled since originally printed. The editors who chose them in different versions cannot be blamed for any alterations.

Thanks to Robert Crawford and Peter Davison for helpful criticism.

"Pont Mirabeau" (in "Two from Apollinaire") first appeared in *French Leave: Translations* (1983); other work was collected in *Winter Thunder* (1990). Both chapbooks were published by Robert L. Barth.

X. J. Kennedy's first collection of poems, *Nude Descending a Staircase* (1961), won the Lamont Award of the Academy of American Poets. His most recent collection, *Cross Ties: Selected Poems* (1985), received the *Los Angeles Times* book award for poetry. Kennedy's other awards for poetry include a Guggenheim fellowship, the Shelley Memorial Award (shared with Mary Oliver), the Golden Rose of the New England Poetry Club, the Michael Braude award of the American Academy and Institute of Arts and Letters, a National Council on the Arts and Humanities grant, and the Bess Hokin Prize of *Poetry* magazine. His verse has appeared in more than three hundred magazines and anthologies. Kennedy has also written ten children's books and several widely adopted college textbooks, including *An Introduction to Poetry*. He lives in Bedford, Massachusetts, with his wife, Dorothy, and four of their five children.